POETIVITIES

GUIDING CREATIVE POETIC EXPRESSION SUCCESSFULLY IN THE ELEMENTARY GRADES

PRIMARY LEVEL

by James Wainwright

illustrated by Paul Manktelow

Cover by Jeff Van Kanegan

Copyright © Good Apple, Inc., 1989

ISBN No. 0-86653-484-9

Good Apple, Inc.
A Division of Frank Schaffer Publications, Inc.
23740 Hawthorne Boulevard,
Torrance, CA 90505-5927

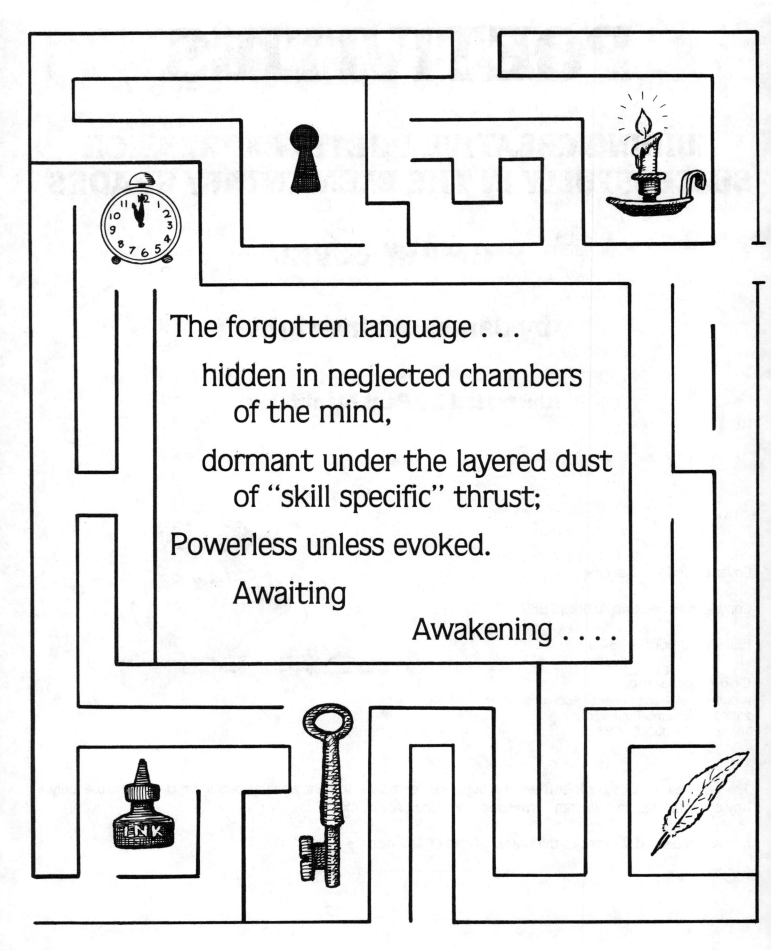

The forgotten language . . .

hidden in neglected chambers
of the mind,

dormant under the layered dust
of "skill specific" thrust;

Powerless unless evoked.

Awaiting

Awakening . . . .

GA1089

Table of Contents

Introduction iv
Poetry: Misunderstood Child of Communication vii
The Trash Compactor viii
Prewriting x
Writing Poetry in the Primary Grades.................xi
Toy Parade 1
Sounds Abound 3
Something's Fishy 6
The BL Monster 9
Where Am I? 12
Flying Free 16
It's a Secret...19
Synonym Cookies...21
How Do You Feel?..24
Cloud Dancing 27
Your Nature Is My Nature 30
What's Your Game? 34
A Day in the Life 37
Who Are You?...42
The Reasons of the Seasons...........................45
For Consideration...50

GA1089

Introduction

Poetivities, a self-created word synthesized from poetry and activities, is an effort to stress the concept that poetry is a skill and, therefore, can be taught.

Each of us is born with much more than an innate desire to communicate our environmental situational experiences. We also seek an avenue for creative expression by which we can communally share the creative expression of our innermost thoughts, dreams, beliefs, feelings, and enigmas. We seek to move another's soul as well as register another's cognitive recognition. Poetry is one of the vehicles that allows us to fulfill this desire.

It is therefore an educational imperative that creative expression in young children be nurtured and developed. A true education must not only serve the logical practicalities of man's functioning within the framework of nature. and society, but must also provide an awakening and involvement in the philosophical and metaphysical questions that have underlined mankind's existence from the very start. Poetry is the metaphorical language that bridges man's perceptions of reality with a greater reality beyond mere sensory data.

The plethora of self-help books and talk show topics often can be distilled into a single problematic realization—that mankind has lost the ability to creatively communicate its inner spirit, getting mired down in the restraints of coexisting in a cognition-based technological society.

GA1089

This book is a guide to unlock the forgotten language of poetic free verse. It is comprised of multi-step lessons designed for the free thinking, free wheeling teacher who seeks to guide very young children into creative expression. It is a developed "idea book" and, like any good manual, should soon be filled with your own personal notes, as teaching, like learning, is not a single-path, static journey but rather an ever changing revisionary as well as visionary process.

I have merely provided a series of field-tested ideas. To utilize this handbook efficiently, you will want to instill your own individual essence into each developed exercise—noting what worked well, what could be expanded, what could be refined for you as an individual. As teachers, if we're not constantly involved in the struggle to reinvent the wheel, then we're destined to roll only so fast, only so smooth, and only on roads on which we feel safe.

The Poetivity lessons are also carefully designed to provide integration primarily in language arts, but also in cross-curriculum disciplines as well. The lessons, particularly the Prewrite Activities, will strengthen grammatical components skills far better than handfuls of English book pages and dittos in that they evoke application from within rather than mere recognition from without.

GA1089

The lessons and the high degree of involvement that they generate will certainly stimulate vocabulary enrichment and will serve to strengthen reading skills, particularly in inferential comprehension. They will also coincide with many of the standard curriculum objectives covered in most science and social studies units typically taught at the elementary level.

Finally, and probably most importantly, *Poetivities* will help break down the invisible barriers of poetry confusion and poetry resistance so common in children. It will subtlely lead your students into both an awareness of poetry's flexible intents and an appreciation of poetry's art.

GA1089

Poetry: Misunderstood Child of Communication

Preconceptions and misinformation have prevented the successful teaching of poetry writing for years. Poetry has mistakenly been looked upon as some kind of quasi-spiritual expression of elitist souls conceived by tormented minds and understood solely by literary intellectuals.

This is both tragic and completely wrong.

Poetry is actually our first venture into shared language expression. Toddlers speak in clipped syntax that is often symbolic of greater meaning than the mere word coupling. *Juice*, for example, actually stands for the unstated meaning of, "I'm thirsty and would like to drink some juice to rid myself of this thirst." This is the very heart of poetry—condensed linguistic lexicons that represent both hidden and multi-level semantical meaning.

The toddler is successful at it and never loses this ability with the infusion of sentence structure. Simply put, the elementary teacher needs only to strip this imposed structure and return to the language foundation in order to insure excellent poetic expression.

This manual will expand upon the simplistic premise stated above and offer devices, methods, and ideas to generate an exciting poetry writing experience for children of all ages.

GA1089

The Trash Compactor

Analogies often clarify foggy new information. In fact, we process all incoming knowledge dependent on our preexisting knowledge base.

Unfortunately, for most children, the preexisting knowledge base in poetry consists solely of Mother Goose and similar silly sing-songy rhymes. This, in turn, makes it somewhat difficult to redirect the thinking of poetic expression in a child who is well-conditioned in these established rhyme and meter patterns. This is not to say that these forms don't play a valid role in child development, but just as a child's dinner menu should reflect some nutritional variety, so too should his literary menu.

The analogy of the trash compactor works well in giving new poetic direction. It is also quite an accurate simplified analogy.

A trash compactor merely alters the form of the collected rubbish. It condenses the volume but in no way alters or eliminates the contents.

Poetry has the same action on prose. It greatly condenses the volume, but it in no way alters or eliminates the intended meaning. Thought and mood that might take five pages to develop and illuminate might effectively be communicated in a poem of five lines.

And, just as the weight of compacted trash is intensified into a smaller area, so too is the power and impact of poetry intensified into a significantly smaller area. This is one of the prime factors that gives poetry the intellectual and emotional "knockout punch" effect.

GA1089

The "trash compactor" concept can be initiated and grasped at an early age. The younger grades will obviously require a physical demonstration of the concept, but by third grade mere verbalization should suffice. By establishing this understanding, you have created a foundation that poetic masterpieces can be erected upon, and I guarantee you won't believe the powerful poetry that your students will generate.

We teachers are but guides along the pathway to creativity, but it pays to have a flashlight along the way.

GA1089

Prewriting

All of the poetry writing activities or "Poetivities" as I refer to them, begin with prewriting activities. Simply stated, prewriting provides the direction, focus, and springboard for the successful completion of any writing task. It is not only a prudent approach, but it is actually essential if writing energy and productivity is to be achieved.

Prewriting is analogous to a baseball pitcher warming up before the actual game, to an engine idling before being run on a cold winter day, to an actor rehearsing a scene before it's shot.

A blank piece of paper and a vague general writing task is quite an obstacle, even for a fluid, experienced writer. A writer must know where he's going, how to get there, and how to get the ballpoint rolling so to speak. Parameters need to be established, and strategies need to be devised. Writing is at best a difficult task; it embraces any assistance it can receive.

This is the area where teaching skills are best utilized. The teacher in prewriting sets the purpose, guides the process, and motivates the outcome. Successful prewriting practically guarantees successful final writing.

The prewriting steps within the "Poetivities" are really nothing more than calculated compasses, generators, and catalysts. They create a positive atmosphere of unity while simultaneously insuring the grasping of the intended concept or task and its subsequent completion. No one hits a bull's-eye without first taking aim.

Writing Poetry in the Primary Grades

The need to communicate is never stronger than it is in the first seven years of a child's life. It is compounded by the enigma of having a racing thought-filled mind that is often stymied by language constraints. The words are just not always there.

By realizing the struggle between communicative enthusiasm and frustration, the teacher can begin to bridge the gap and minimize internal negativism. Most teachers of primary grade children are masters at this bridging technique. They provide frequent oral opportunities and often utilize parents or upper grade children in story transcription.

The following "Poetivities" often revolve around a group participatory piece. This provides a thought-word interactive process in which all the children can feel connected, and, in fact, they each share in the success of the final product making them equal authors and imprinting future language manipulation.

negativism

Also, since poem construction is not harnessed by "right or wrong" responses, the freedom and ease for sharing is very high, and embarrassment becomes virtually nonexistent.

Primary grade teachers are the hardest working, most gifted, and most important teachers within the educational system. You'll have a classroom full of poets in no time.

GA1089

POETIVITIES

"Yea, though I walk through the valley of the shadow of death...."

"In Xanadu did Kubla Khan A stately pleasure-dome decree...."

"I think that I shall never see...."

"Double, Double Toil and Trouble...."

"I took the one less traveled by, And that has made all the difference."

Toy Parade

Poetry Objective: Free expression/Formatting

Language Objective: Noun-verb relationships/Word endings

Reading Objective: Classifying objects

Prewrite Activities

1. Bring a Teddy bear to class.

2. Discuss the part that toys play in our lives.

3. Share all the things that you can do with your bear.
   Example: hold, cuddle, wave, kiss, dance, etc.

Toy Parade

1. Have each child bring his favorite toy to class.

2. Create a "group poem" on the board.
   Setup: Tell children you're going to pretend that the toys they brought in are going to be part of a big toy parade.

   The contents of the poem merely will be the toy mentioned, followed by an action that the toy would do.

   Be sure to print it on the board in stacked lines.

1

Example:
The doll smiled,
The truck honked,
The baseball bounced,
The monkey jumped,
The soldier saluted,
The baby cried,
The gun fired,
The doggie barked,
All in the toy parade.

Be sure to include every child's toy and to use their ideas. Chime in only when the class is stuck. Guide them in word choice if duplication and repetition arise. They know many synonyms without realizing it.

Expansion Ideas

1. Introduce the concept of descriptive writing (adjectives) by going back and inserting a word that describes the toy.

2. Place all the toys on a large table and group them by similar features.

3. Generate numerous creative writing opportunities with the table full of toys. (Tell about a toy party . . . pretend all the toys were as big as children and came to life . . . if toys had feelings, what would a typical "toy day" be like?)

2

Sounds Abound

Poetry Objective: Sensory awareness

Language Objective: Word creation (introduction to onomatopoeia)

Reading Objective: To show how action is sometimes expressed so as to make the intended experience more vivid and real. Vowel sounds/consonant blends.

Prewrite Activities

1. Find and play an album of sound effects. (If not in your library/ learning center, most public libraries will have one.)

2. Pick selected album sounds and attempt to write them on the board.

    Example: The sound of a race car motor,

    Vvvvrrrrrooooommmm . . . errrrrooom

    Have *fun* with it. You're dealing with sounds, not words.

3. Lead into the generation of an onomatopoeia word list (crack, boom, bang, drip, etc.).

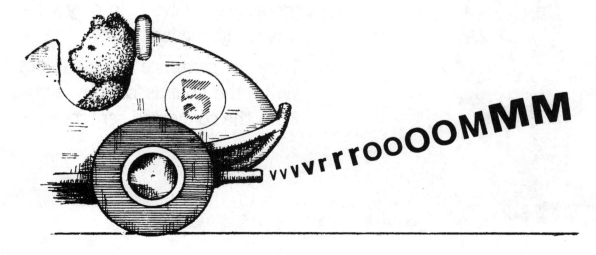

GA1089

Sounds Abound

1. Have the following sentence story on the board:
   a. Andy and Randy were crying because they were lost in the woods.
   b. It was getting dark and the wind began to blow.
   c. Off in the distance, they heard a coyote.
   d. An owl called from a tree.
   e. It started to storm.
   f. They ran through the leaves and sticks as fast as they could.
   g. They were tired and breathing heavily.
   h. Andy fell into a big puddle.
   i. Randy cut his arm on a branch and yelled in pain.
   j. Their friend Sandy fired three shots into the air to help them find their way back.
   k. They ran towards the sounds and when they spotted the cabin they cheered.
   l. They ran inside and shut the door very hard.
   m. Andy and Randy went straight to bed and fell asleep.

2. Next to these sentences, translate the story into a Sound Poem. Be sure to have at least one sound for each sentence.

   Have the children create this group piece. Give help only when it is really needed.

   Take it sentence by sentence. Write the sounds directly across from the connected sentences.

4

GA1089

The completed poem should look something like this:

                Lost and Found
Waaaaa . . .
Wewwww . . . Swishhhhhhhhhhh . . .
Arr . . . arr . . . arr . . . aroooooooo . . .
Whoooo . . . whoooo . . .
Crack . . . Ba . . . Boom!
Crunch . . . crunch . . . crackle . . . Snap . . .
Huhh . . . huhh . . . whewww . . .
SPLASH!
Owwwwwwww!!!!
Bang! Bang! Bang!
Yea . . .
Slam!
Zzzzzzzzzzzzzz . . . .

Expansion Ideas

1. After sharing the story poem, discuss why the poem version is more exciting.

2. Have the children put it on tape. They'll have a ball doing it and listening to it.

3. Older primary classes can break into small groups and create their own Sound Poems.

GA1089

Something's Fishy

Poetry Objective: Relating and expressing the external

Language Objective: Word associations

Reading Objective: Personification/Point of view

Prewrite Activities

1. Do a group pantomime where students act out a variety of animals (dog, lion, rabbit, snake). After each pantomime, discuss what kind of things *might* be going through the animal's mind.

2. Read "Goldilocks and the Three Bears." List the ways the bears act like people (a lesson in personification). . . . family unit . . . live in a house with furniture . . . speak . . . cook . . . think . . . .

3. Discuss the story from the bears' point of view, emphasizing that they were merely minding their own business, going about their normal lives, when Goldilocks actually broke into their house, (crime), stole their food, (crime), and broke their personal belongings, (crime). Generate a brainstorming discussion on what the bears might have thought and what the bears might have felt.

4. Arrange to have a goldfish in a fishbowl for the students to observe and either distribute the following sheet or do together on the board.

Goldie

Thinks About

Gets Happy About

Pretends

Thinks About

7

Something's Fishy

1. Take the "fish notes" and compose a group goldfish thought poem.

   Example:

   Inside Goldie's Mind

   What are these people staring at?
   > I'm bored . . . .
   >> I'm lonely.

   This food tastes like paper!
   > Hope my gold is gleaming.

   Least there's no fisherman to bother me.

2. Brainstorm a list of all the fish the students know.

3. Their task is to write a poem from their chosen fish's point of view, speculating on what its thoughts may be. (Odds are that the vast majority of boys in particular will choose the shark, so try to make other fish sound interesting in the setup.)

Expansion Ideas

1. Coordinate poetivity with a science unit on fish.

2. Make papier-mâché fish to go with their poems.

3. Arrange a field trip to a local aquarium if possible.

4. Put an aquarium in the room and create an interest center to go with it.

The BL Monster

Poetry Objective: Working with sounds

Language Objective: Alliteration

Reading Objective: Consonant blends

Prewrite Activities

1. Concentrate current reading skills on consonant blends.

2. Have children draw and color large made-up monsters.

3. Do some fun tongue twisters with the class to reinforce beginning sound repetition (alliteration).

   Example:
   Loud lazy Larry loves licking luscious licorice lollipops.

9

4. Give each child his own consonant blend.

5. This is a great opportunity for a dictionary experience as you have the students use the dictionary to create word lists for their blends.

6. Students are then to use their word lists and create blend poems for their monsters.

Expansion Ideas

1. Team children with a partner and have them combine their monsters to create a story or play.

2. Have the children create their own tongue twisters.

3. Put the pictures and poems together into a class book.

4. Create make-believe background information for the monsters.

5. Have the students give names to their monsters and for one entire day use the monster names to call on the children.

The BL Monster

1. Take the monster that *you* drew and tape it on the front chalkboard.

2. Call it the BL Monster.

3. Create a group poem that uses as many BL blends as possible.

4. It will probably be necessary in the earlier grades to begin with BL word lists.

Example: black, blast, blaze, bleed, blind, blink, blob, block, blood, blow, blue, blur

BL Monster
Black and blue blockhead,
A big blue blob,
Blinking blind eyes that blur,
A mouth that blows blazing fire
And blasts away blue blood enemies.

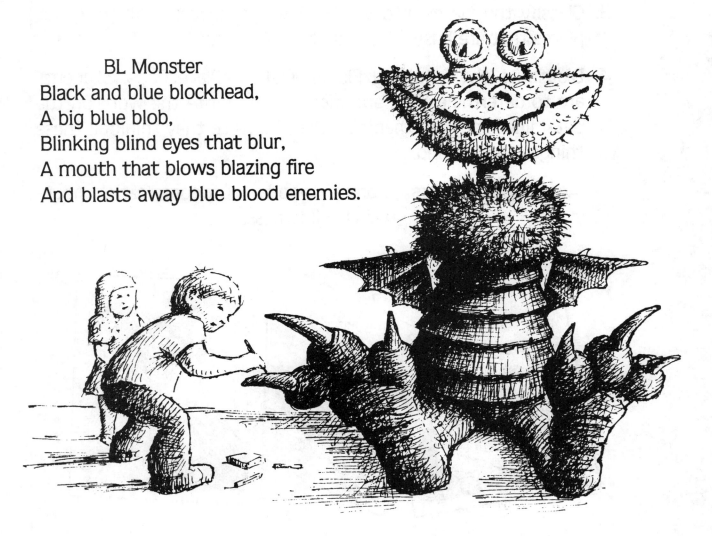

GA1089

Where Am I?

Poetry Objective: Word choosing/Condensing

Language Objective: Nouns

Reading Objective: Establishing clues to setting

Prewrite Activities

1. Have each child share his favorite place during share time or show and tell.

2. Have a variety of pictures of places available.

3. Classify the places into similar features (places that are quiet, places that are busy, places that are fun, etc.).

4. Distribute the following Flower Outline/Place Page. Students are to determine the petal pictures and write the word on the petal line. They are then to write the place they think all these things can be found.

   Acceptable Answers: Forest, woods, outdoors, park, mountains, wilderness.

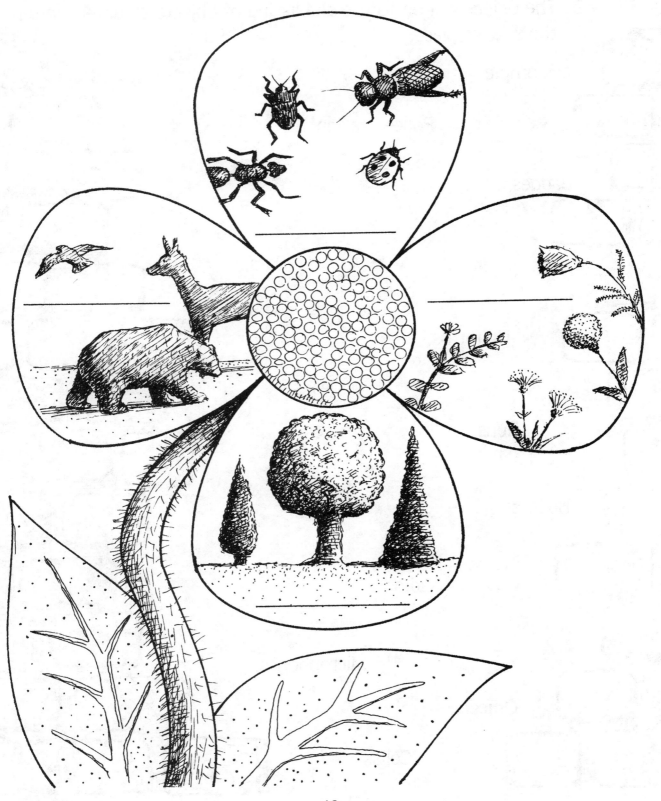

13

Where Am I?

1. Put the following poem on the board without the title.

2. The object will be to use the listing of objects to determine the specific place.

Example:

A Police Station

Badges,

Bars,

Uniforms,

Desks,

Guns,

Bullets,

Radios,

Microphones,

Officers,

Cells.

14

3. Upon sharing the group poem, give children their own individual places to work with (amusement parks, playgrounds, zoos, supermarkets, schools, museums, airports, etc.).

4. They are to write in a free-form fashion objects that are found in their particular places.

5. Children take turns sharing their poems as classmates guess the places.

Expanion Ideas

1. Have the children go back and put describing words in front of the nouns in their poems (adjectives).

2. Convert the noun poems into picture poems.

3. Create a favorite place bulletin board, complete with pictures and poems.

4. Have children do similar exercises using the various rooms in their houses.

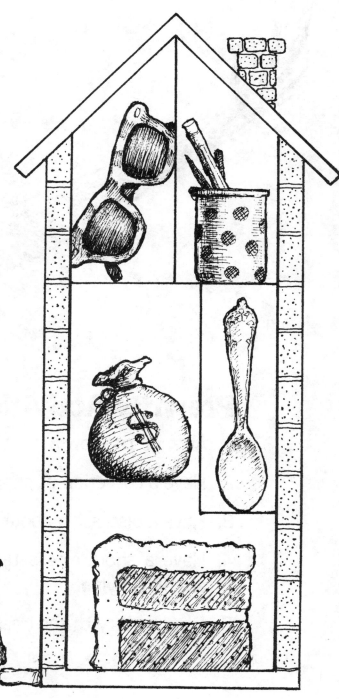

Flying Free

Poetry Objective: Developing out-of-experience expression/ Creating mood

Language Objective: Word building (suffixes)/Adjectives, verbs

Reading Objective: Comprehending character actions

Prewrite Activities

1. Arrange to show a movie/filmstrip of birds in flight.

2. Have a collection of photographs of birds available.

3. Have a discussion about what it would be like to fly.

4. Have a short recess time in which the children pretend they are birds flying.

5. Read a story to the class about birds.

16

Flying Free

1. Turn the lights out and have the children either sit on top of their desks or lie on their backs on the floor, if you have carpeting.

2. Tell the children they are birds.

3. They are to describe how and what they are feeling as they fly through the skies.

4. Transcribe what they share. Try to guide them into the use of all of their senses.

Possible Outcome:

Up into the beautiful skies.
Wind blowing around my wings,
As I float and glide above the trees.
The noisy town far below doesn't even notice me.
The air is cool and crisp and smells wonderful.
It is so fresh.
I roll and twist in the breeze,
Such fun!
I love it.
I want to fly forever and ever,
The sky is my friend.

Expansion Ideas

1. Tie the flying poems in with some bird artwork.

2. Have the class make paper wings and beaks and have a Bird Day in school.

3. Read them one of the numerous children's books that has a bird as a central character.

4. Tie in with a short science introduction to the many different kinds of birds and the way they live.

5. Pick a selection of some of the most popular birds in the class and make a bridge to geography by either pinning or taping little bird cutouts onto a map, reinforcing where a particular type of bird can be found.

6. Create a bird interest center.

7. Make a bulletin board depicting all the various birds that are on the endangered species list.

GA1089

It's a Secret

Poetry Objective:
   To build to a greater unstated meaning

Language Objective:
   Word choice

Reading Objective:
   Associations/Sequence/Subtle introduction to inference

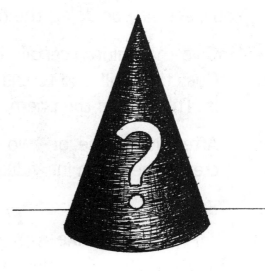

Prewrite Activities

1. Do some standard riddles with the children.
    Example: What's black and white and "red" all over?
                    A newspaper!

2. Have some large jigsaw style cutouts of various items. Present one piece at a time, and have children guess at what it is.

3. Tell small selected bits of well-known children's stories, and have children guess what story it is.
    Example: This sure is a long walk . . . . Where are you going? . . . The woods are dangerous . . . . The dentist should get a look at those big teeth . . . . Get your axe, Woodcutter . . . . I want my Grandma!

GA1089

It's a Secret

You'll actually be doing the reverse of the prewrite activities.

1. Give the children certain items and have them construct phrase clues that will lead to the final understanding of what the object is. This will be the poem.

2. After doing one or two group clue poems, have the children create their own individual poems.

   Example:

   A Bike

   Rolling along,
   Chain whipping around,
   Rubber skidding on clean pave-
   ment,
   Feet pushing hard on the pedals,
   Racing fast.

Expansion Ideas

1. Have children pretend they are famous story, movie, or cartoon characters, and slowly leak clues as to their identities.

2. Have them write similar poems about themselves and/or family members.

GA1089

Synonym Cookies

Poetry Objective: Word choice (for intended meanings, and sound qualities)

Language/Reading Objective: Introduction to synonyms

Prewrite Activities

1. Share similar branching words. Arrange to have an ice cube for each child to hold. Starting with the basic word *cold*, get the students to generate a list of words that mean "cold."

2. Discuss with the class what synonyms are and share the subtle differences in the words of their lists. Be sure to talk about the differences in the word sounds and the differences in the strength of word meanings.

   (Example: Which word is stronger, *cold* or *freezing*?)

3. Distribute the following outline picture of an elephant. Brainstorm and list all the words the class can come up with that mean "big." (*enormous, large, huge, magnificent, stupendous, humongous, gigantic*, etc.)

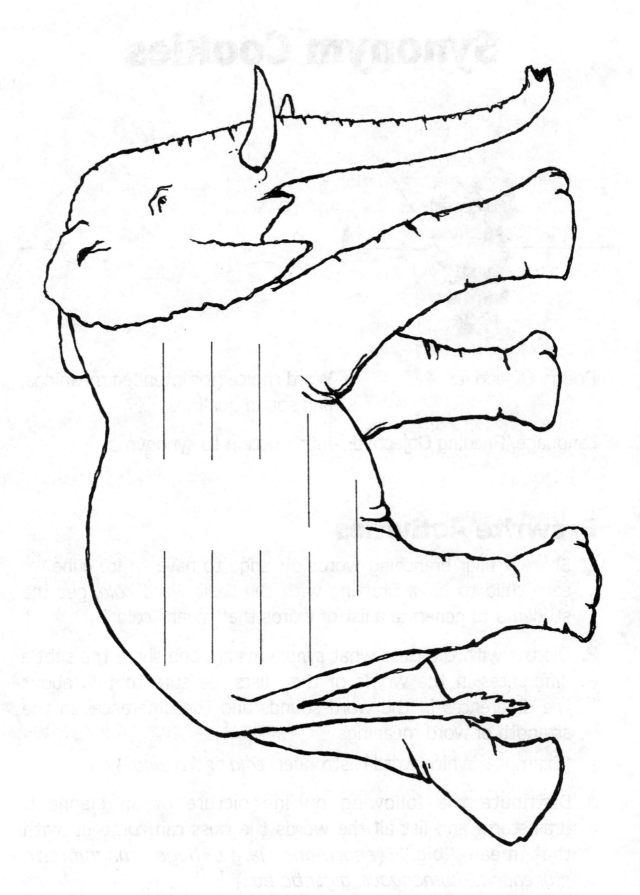

Synonym Cookies

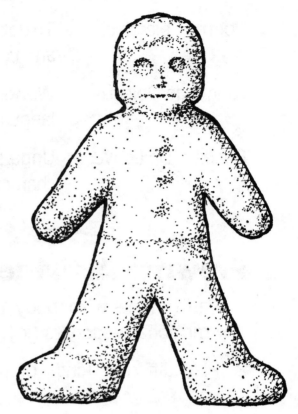

1. Make cookies with the class. Give each student some wax paper and cookie dough and have him shape the dough in whatever form he chooses. Then bake the cookies.

2. Give each student his baked cookie and have him draw a picture of it. The picture should be twice the size. Tell him that he should try to make the cookie picture look exactly like his cookie, complete with bumps, wrinkles, browned edges, etc.

3. Have the students eat the cookies.

4. Have the students write synonyms for the cookie's taste around the edges of their drawn cookies. Begin them with the word *good*.

Expansion Ideas

1. Have them cut pictures out of magazines and do a similar write-around-the-edges activity.

2. Create Synonym Notebooks as a class.

3. Extend the cookie activity by having them write similes for the cookie through all five senses.

   Example: My cookie looks like . . . a tiny mountain.

GA1089

How Do You Feel?

Poetry Objective: To get in touch with emotional understanding and communicate the mood and feeling

Language Objective: Working with expressive and descriptive language

Reading Objective: Understanding character traits/Explaining character actions based on character feeling

Prewrite Activities

1. Pantomime with body language and facial expressions basic emotional responses (joy, sadness, anger, etc.).

2. Play different kinds of music and relate it to how it makes you *feel*.

3. Read the following situations and talk about how they would make you feel. Have the students put on the appropriate facial expressions as well.

24

a. A bully just broke your favorite toy.

b. You just got a new bike for your birthday.

c. Your dog Bosco just died.

d. You are next in line for Space Mountain at Disney World.

e. You just dropped a big chocolate milk shake in your lap.

f. Your best friend in the whole world just moved far away.

How Do You Feel?

1. Turn the lights off and have children put their heads down.

2. Tell them we're going to drift back in time using our memories.

3. Give them an emotional response and force them to concentrate on a personal experience that is connected to that feeling (fear, anger, joy).

GA1089

4. After about a minute of quiet concentration, turn the lights back on and have children write poems about their memories.

Rule One: No rhymes

Rule Two: No more than three words on a line

Put the following example on the board as a guide:

Worried

Big dentist office
White and scary
Loud drills
Will I gag
Will it hurt
I'm scared
Please, God,
A good checkup
today
OK.

Expansion Ideas

1. To get the children comfortable with the loose structure of poems, have them write their scattered words around shape pictures. (A big heart for a love poem, a big smile for a happy poem, big bulging eyes for a scared poem, etc.)

2. Keep "feelings" diaries in the room.

3. Utilize the groundwork for positive student interaction with regard to one another's feelings.

GA1089

Cloud Dancing

Poetry Objective: Imagery

Language Objective: Descriptive writing

Reading Objective: Associations

Prewrite Activities

1. Using large construction paper, create a bunch of ink blots by dropping a "glob" of paint/ink in the center and folding and pressing.

2. Hold up the *large* ink blots one at a time and elicit responses from the class as to what images they see. (Be sure to turn the blot pictures in different directions as you do this.)

3. Have children take out plain pieces of white paper and black crayons. They are to close their eyes and wildly scribble as you count off, "One thousand one, one thousand two, one thousand three, STOP!"

4. Students are then to write their names on the backs of their scribble sheets.

5. Have the students then, on separate pieces of paper, write down descriptions of what they see in the scribbles.

                    GA1089

6. Collect the "scribbles" and redistribute them in the class so that each child gets someone else's scribble.

7. On another sheet of paper they are to write what they see in this new scribble.

8. When they are finished, they are to return what they wrote and the scribble to the original artist, who will then compare what he wrote with what his classmate wrote.

9. Follow up with a discussion on why they think people see different images in nonspecific art.

Cloud Dancing

1. Pick a day when the sky is full of thick, fluffy, white clouds.

2. Have the students get pencils and notebooks, and take them outside to cloud stare.

3. Every time they see a particular image in a cloud or cloud formation, they are to write down what they see, adding as much specific descriptive detail as possible.

28

It will be absolutely imperative for you to get them started with some "high-rev" modeling.

Example:

I see a fat, toothless, one-eared hippopotamus with a dragon's tail sitting on a beach ball . . . .

4. Back in the classroom, each student takes his notes and writes them on a large sheet of construction paper in any order or form he chooses, under the title of "Cloud Dancing."

5. Have the students decorate their "Cloud Dancing" by gluing cotton balls as three-dimensional clouds.

Expansion Ideas

1. Tie in to an art lesson in modern art/surrealistic art.

2. A similar technique can be used to combine finger painting with creative writing.

3. Write a class story about some mythological cloud kingdom.

4. Do a science mini-lesson on clouds and their types and formations.

Your Nature Is My Nature

Poetry Objective: Imagery/Mood

Language Objective: Descriptive writing/Adjectives

Reading Objective: Similes/Sensory comprehension

Prewrite Activities

This Poetivity dovetails with the standard nature awareness aspect inherent in most primary curriculums.

1. Have a discussion on what it means to be observant.

2. Arrange to have a fellow teacher/administrator stop in the room for a moment.

3. After the adult leaves the room, have the children write down everything they can about the person's looks and clothes.

4. Share and reinforce the concept of observation.

5. Give each child a Ziploc bag and take the entire class on a nature hike around the building. Children are to find and place the following items in their bags: grass, leaves, bark, stones, weeds, flower petals.

6. Students use their nature "stuff" to fill in the following sheets (Observations Revisited).

GA1089

Observations Revisited

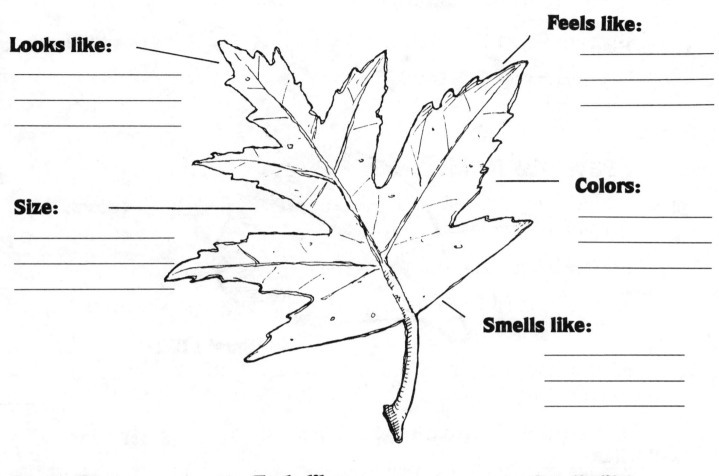

Looks like:

_____

_____

_____

_____

Feels like:

_____

_____

_____

Size: _____

_____

_____

_____

Colors:

_____

_____

_____

Smells like:

_____

_____

_____

Looks like:

_____

_____

Feels like:

_____

_____

Smells like:

_____

_____

Size: _____

_____

_____

Colors:

_____

_____

GA1089

Observations Revisited

Looks like:

_____

_____

_____

Feels like:

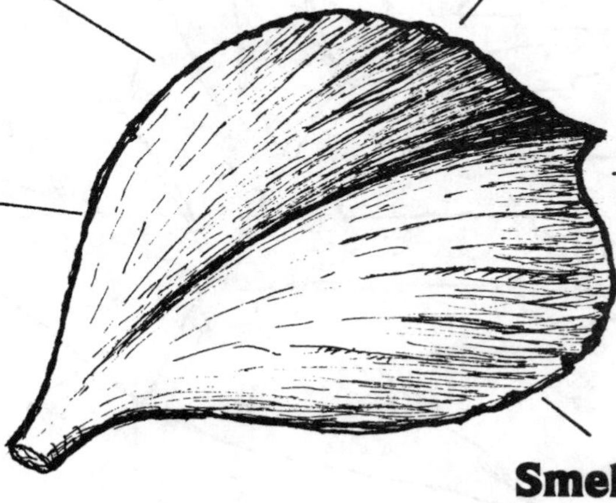

_____

_____

_____

Size:

_____

_____

_____

Colors:

_____

_____

_____

Smells like:

_____

_____

_____

Looks like:

_____

_____

_____

Feels like:

_____

_____

_____

Smells like:

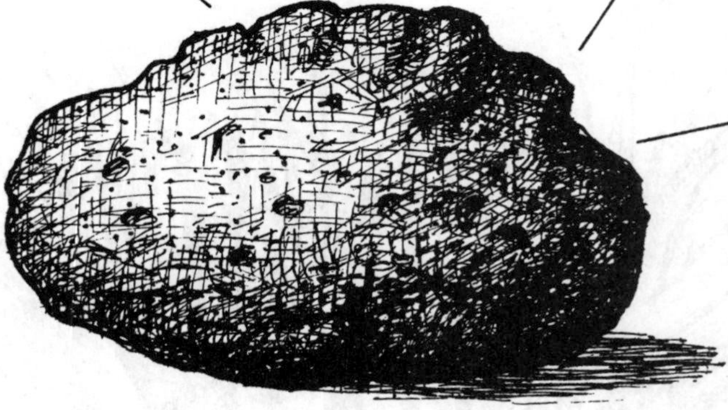

_____

_____

Size:

_____

_____

_____

Colors:

_____

_____

_____

GA1089

Your Nature Is My Nature

1. Give each student a large sheet of manila drawing paper and have him draw an outdoor nature scene. (It should include all the elements of his Ziploc bag collection.)

   Students' pictures should *not* have man or anything man-made in them and should have *plenty* of blank uncolored sections in them.

2. Students are then to select the simile parts of their nature sheets and write them in the blank spaces of their pictures.

3. Display the pictures and immediately break into a lesson on similes.

Expansion Ideas

1. Integrate a science unit on plants or rocks.

2. Create a Simile Notebook with similes and corresponding pictures.

   Examples:

   My baby brother/sister is like a _____.

   My bedroom is like a _____.

   Recess is like a _____.

What's Your Game?

Poetry Objective: Inferential clues

Language Objective: Specific nouns/Verbs

Reading Objective: Word associations/Sequence

Prewrite Activities

1. Have a shared discussion on favorite nonsport games. Follow up with a brainstorming discussion on the value and importance of games. (Why are they fun? What do they teach us? Etc.)

2. Distribute Bingo cards and beans and play a few games of Bingo.

3. Write *Bingo* on the board and discuss how, although really a game of luck, there are "brain benefits." Write *Number/Letter Recognition* and *Listening Skills* on the board.

4. Make two columns on the board: *Nouns   Verbs*

5. Under the Nouns column, brainstorm and list the "things" necessary to play Bingo: cards, beans, spinner/tumbler, tiles, caller.

6. Under the Verbs column, brainstorm and list the "actions" that take place during a Bingo game: spin, call, listen, look, pick, place, fill, win, shout.

34

7. Combine the words into a noun/verb poem being sure to string together the appropriate combinations.

Example:

Bingo

Caller spins,

Caller calls,

Players listen and look,

Beans picked,

Beans placed,

Column filled,

Player shouts,

Player wins.

Emphasize how the understanding of the game is conveyed in a mere handful of words.

What's Your Game?

1. Have a variety of fairly simple board/card games available for class playing.

2. Divide the class into groups of three or four and distribute the games, avoiding duplication if possible.

3. Groups play their game and as a group repeat the prewriting activity of listing the nouns (things) and verbs (actions) in labeled columns.

 GA1089

4. Each group is then responsible to turn their selected words into a poem format similar to Bingo. Try to emphasize the order of the actions (sequencing).

5. After the games are collected and the poems are composed, each group shares their poem without mention of the game as other groups guess.

Expansion Ideas

1. Further develop the clipped game poems by the addition of information words (adjectives/adverbs). Use "Bingo" as your example.

Bingo
Caller spins rapidly,
Caller calls clearly,
 Anxious players listen carefully,
 And look quickly,
 Shiny beans picked,
 Slippery beans placed,
Diagonal column filled,
 Excited player shouts wildly,
 Happy player wins.

2. More advanced students can be given cardboard, dice, and playing pieces and as a group create their own game and their own poem.

B I N G O

3	65	7	12	34
50	49	23	4	67

A Day in the Life

Poetry Objective: Personification/Point of view

Language Objective: Writing to a defined purpose

Reading Objective: Character traits/Character motivation

Prewrite Activities

1. This poetry exercise dovetails beautifully with a unit study on animals and especially a trip to the local zoo.

2. Have an activity/interest center where the children get the opportunity to receive as much information on various wild animals as possible.

3. Lead a discussion on the children's favorite animals, being sure to draw specific reasons for their choices.

4. Do a short class charades game with children acting out various wild animals.

5. Have the children make lists of ten wild animals that they think they know a lot about (a good time to introduce the concept of prioritized listing).

37

A Day in the Life

1. Take the children's lists of animals and circle one, making sure to get a wide range of variety in the room.

2. After all the children have received their animals, have them close their eyes and turn the lights off. Guide the class into forgetting themselves, and, using the full power of their imaginations, they are to lock in to what it would be like if they were indeed their chosen animals. Give them frequent auditory clues so they really "lock in" on the particular setting where their animals would be found so that they fully visualize their surroundings.

3. Turn the lights back on while reinforcing that they are to stay in character.

4. Pass out the following animal information sheet. The students are to fill in the information as accurately as possible. Offer assistance when needed, and it would be a good idea to have the library's complete set of zoo books if possible (introduction to research).

GA1089

Animal Information

Type of animal: _____

Animal's first name: _____

Animal's last name: _____

Animal's home: _____

Animal's favorite food: _____

Animal's enemies: _____

_____

Picture of Animal

_____

Now, as your animal, write about your most interesting or exciting day. _____

_____

_____

_____

_____

_____

_____

GA1089

5. Distribute a sheet of paper broken into fragmented present progressive verbs:

Running through . . . .

        Hiding in . . . .

Eating . . . .

        Playing . . . .

    Watching out for . . . .

Thinking about . . . .

        Dreaming about . . . .

6. Children are to finish the fragmented phrases as they think their animals would answer.

Example:

Running through the jungle

        Hiding in thick tall grass

Eating antelope

        Playing paw tag

    Watching out for hunters

Thinking about my cubs

        Dreaming about being king

GA1089

7. Upon finishing their clipped phrases, the children are to add two to four more "compacted" phrases from their interesting/ exciting experiences activity.

8. Have each child read his finished poem without mentioning the animal, and then have the rest of the class guess the animal.

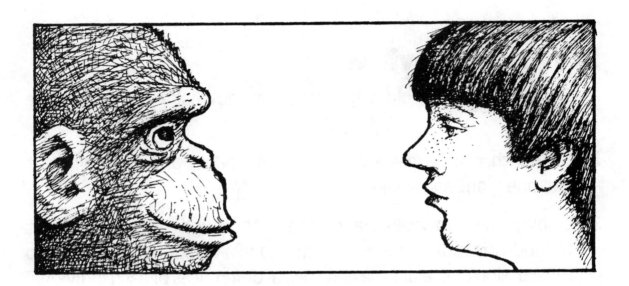

Expansion Ideas

1. Follow up the poetry experience by having the children write mini-reports about their animals, complete with art projects such as clay or papier-mâché models.

2. Have children make little paper cutouts of their animals and pin them to a large map reinforcing their geographical homelands.

3. Generate vocabulary lists on animal groups (herds, prides, flocks, etc.) and animal sounds (growls, roars, whistles, etc.).

4. Have a short late afternoon Animal Party where the children wear paper masks of their animals and eat Animal Crackers.

GA1089

Who Are You?

Poetry Objective: Self-understanding/Self-expression

Language Objective: Nouns/Adjectives

Reading Objective: Semantic word mapping

Prewrite Activities

1. Demonstrate the old tried-and-true snowflake cutout to the class.

2. Give each child a piece of plain white paper and have him cut out one giant snowflake.

3. Display the snowflakes and lead a thorough discussion about the individual differences in each snowflake, springboarding into a discussion of the unique and special differences of each individual person.

4. Select two children to bring up to the front of the class. Have the students brainstorm the various differences between the two, beginning with the obvious physical differences and leading them into recognizing some of the basic differences in their personalities and their individualized likes and dislikes.

5. Give each student the following word mapping sheet. Students fill in their personal information.

GA1089

I Am . . .

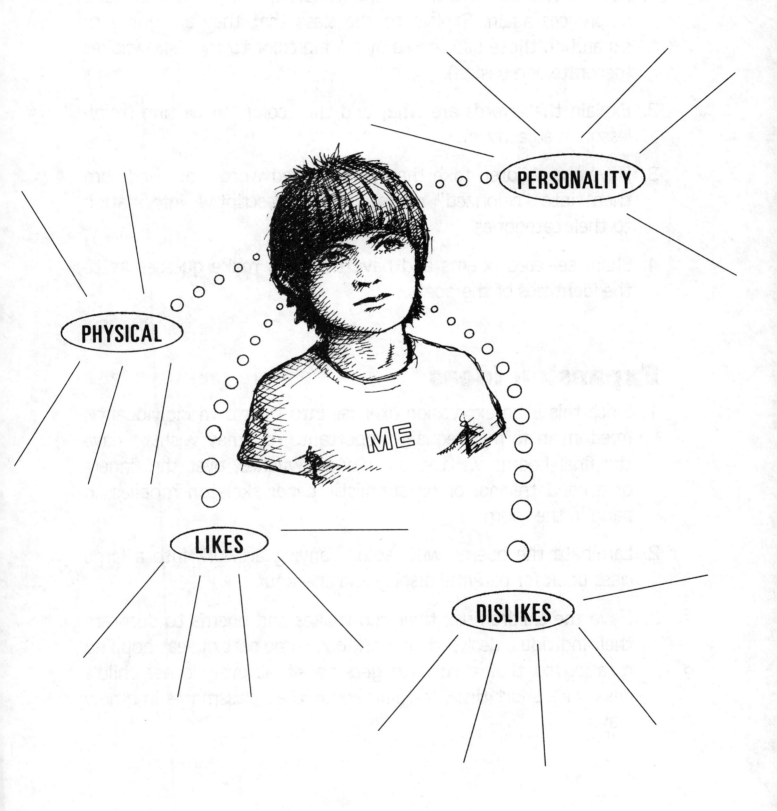

PERSONALITY

PHYSICAL

ME

LIKES

DISLIKES

GA1089

Who Are You?

1. Return the snowflakes to the children, reviewing the basic differences again. Explain to the class that they are going to expand on those differences by adding color to their snowflakes (decorate and design).

2. Explain that words are what add the "color" in writing (mini-lesson in adjectives).

3. Have the children take their personalized word maps and turn them into "colorized" poems, adding descriptive information to their categories.

4. Share selected poems and have the class make guesses as to the identities of the poets.

Expansion Ideas

1. Since this is an expression exercise into their own individuality, freedom in form is equally important. You may wish to have the final poems written on new snowflakes, over the fingers of a hand tracing, or on simplistic paper skeleton mobiles to hang in the room.

2. Laminate the poems with accompanying artwork into a large class book for parental display and checkout.

3. Have the children use their snowflakes and poems to decorate their individual desks; then work out some sort of seat hopping rotation so that each child gets to sit at every other child's desk for a short time, learning about their classmates in a new way.

The Reasons of the Seasons

Poetry Objective: Figurative language

Language Objective: Symbols and connotations

Reading Objective: Categorize specific vocabulary

Prewrite Activities

This Poetivity blends well with lessons involving learning the months and/or science units on weather.

1. Create a four-panel bulletin board with each section labeled one of the four seasons.

    Spring   Summer   Fall   Winter

2. Distribute old magazines used for cutting purposes.

3. Students are to find, cut out, and paste pictures that pertain to a specific season, trying to find at least one picture for each season.

4. When the bulletin board is completed, point to particular cutouts and have that student explain why that picture goes under the selected season.

5. Distribute the following "seasonal pies" and guide the students through their chart fill-ins. Emphasize that what they write down has to be particular to the season.

GA1089

Seasonal Pie

List the different things you do in each season.

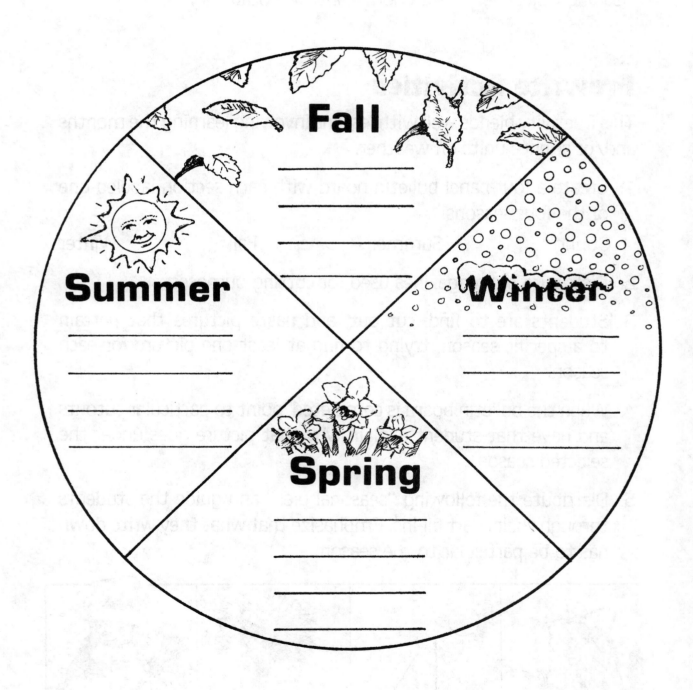

GA1089

Seasonal Pie

List the different things you see in each season.

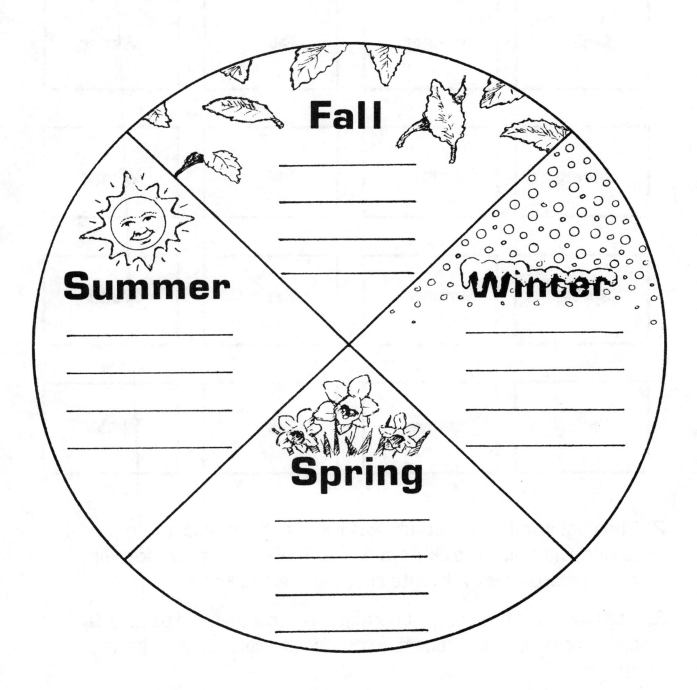

GA1089

The Reasons of the Seasons

1. Duplicate, cut and fold the following secret seasons:

Spring	**Summer**	**Fall**	**Winter**
Spring	**Summer**	**Fall**	**Winter**
Spring	**Summer**	**Fall**	**Winter**
Spring	**Summer**	**Fall**	**Winter**

2. Thoroughly mix the cutout seasons and go around the room having the children pick from a hat. The season they pick will be the season they will write about in their poems.

3. The student is to take the information gathered in the pie charts and weave it into a poem with his particular season as the title.

4. Upon completion, students take turns reading their poems while the class guesses the mystery seasons. (Make a game out of it.)

GA1089

5. Have a post-poem discussion, reemphasizing how chosen select symbols automatically make a person associate with a particular season.

Examples:
sled . . . . winter
swimming pool . . . . summer
football . . . . fall
Easter . . . . spring

Expansion Ideas

1. Use the following ballot to have the students vote for their favorite season (a good experience in backing up an opinion with specific detail).

I cast my vote for the season of _____

This is the best season because _____

_____

_____

_____

_____

2. Do a creative writing/art project on make-believe seasons describing what they would be like.
Sumall (a combination of summer and fall)
Sprinter (a combinaton of spring and winter)

GA1089

For Consideration

Literary style is absorbed through exposure much in the same way that music and art appreciation are developed. One cannot minimize the strength of the oral tradition in seed-planting style variations as well as initiating a motivating interest and appreciation of any form of literature.

This is especially true in regard to poetry, as it is the one literary expression capable of generating such a vast variety of styles and formats. By reading poems to your class, you not only can fill short time gaps, but can open an awareness to thought and feeling that will reflect itself in each child's personal communications.

Again, the key is variety. Many teachers seem to restrict their poetry reading to Shel Silverstein. He is fantastic and entertaining, to be sure, but should definitely be augmented with other forms and intents. Children *do* have a strong capacity for dealing with serious and mood-provoking material; let's not underestimate their hearts, as we certainly can't afford to underestimate their minds.

Sprinkle your poetry reading wisely. In addition to Mr. Silverstein, share some Dickinson, some Poe, some Frost, some Whitman, even some Shakespeare. Even if the meaning is beyond their comprehension, and remember that poetry can be understood at many diverse levels, the richness and musicality of the language itself will seep in more than you could possibly realize.

GA1089

51

GA1089

Teacher: Magician

Illusions . . . .
        Vaporizing the confusions
        with a wave of the wand
                and a puff of smoke

Pulling rabbits out of a hat
                is a snap
        compared to pulling literacy out of a head

The great disappearing act—
        dispelling the substance—less demons
        who go by names as old as time:
        "I don't know how," "I don't get it,"
        "I don't want to," "I don't care"

The great appearing act—
        Replacing the demons with substantial angels
        who go by names as gold as time:
        "Confidence," "Determination,"
        "Enthusiasm," "Understanding"

Let the skeptical hecklers spout
                For we don't doubt
                that we possess the true magic

GA1089